Music Minus One Clarinet

Igor Stravinsky L'Histoire du Soldat

The Soldier's March

Soldier At The Brook

Pastorale

The Royal March

The Little Concert

Three Dances Tango, Waltz, Ragtime

The Devil's Dance

Grand Chorale

Triumphal March Of The Devil

The Soldier's March
Marching Tunes

Printed in Canada

Soldier At The Brook

Pastorale

The Royal March

The Little Concert

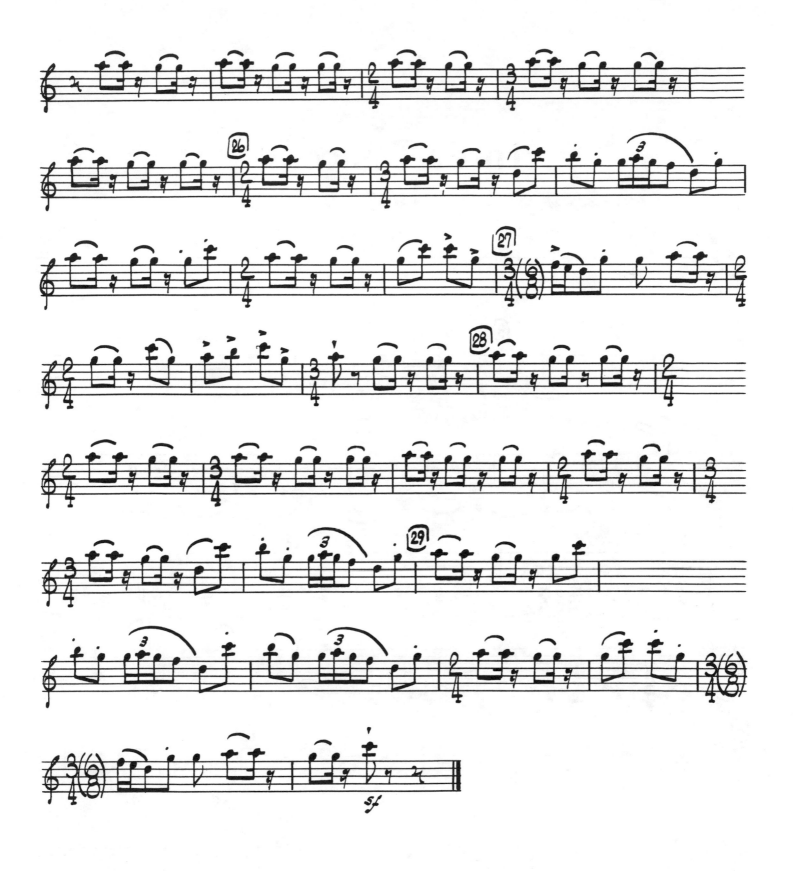

Three Dances
Tango

Segue
to

Waltz

marcato (en dehors)

poco pesante

(simile)

p sub.

sub. >   sub. >   poco   a   poco

cresc.

Segue
to
Ragtime

Ragtime

The Devil's Dance

4 taps (1 meas.) precede music.

Grand Chorale

MMO CD 3217

Triumphal March Of The Devil

(In B♭) M.M. ♩=112   4 taps (1 meas.) precede music.

COMPACT DISC PAGE AND BAND INFORMATION

• WORLD'S LARGEST CATALOGUE OF *Participation Records*

MUSIC MINUS ONE • 43 West 61st Street • New York, N.Y. 10023